THE STORY OF EASTER

Written by Solveig Muus
Illustrations by Jepree Manalaysay

TABLE OF CONTENTS

Library of Congress Control Number: 2011910786
ISBN 978-1-936020-31-7

Jesus Teaches His Disciples

Jesus taught his followers many things. He taught them in ways that were peaceful and forgiving. His most important lesson was that God loved us so much that He sent His beloved Son—Jesus—into the world, to die for all people, to save us from our sins.

The followers of Jesus, who were his apostles and disciples, thought he had come to build an army or become a great king on earth. However, Jesus had come to die, to free all people from their sins. He told his apostles three different times that he would be betrayed by those he loved. He told them he would suffer and die, and that on the third day he would rise from the dead.

Once, Jesus took his three apostles, Peter, James, and John, up onto a high mountain. Suddenly Jesus began to shine like the sun! Even his clothes turned a bright white. He revealed his glory to his apostles. Afterwards, Jesus repeated that he would have to suffer and die, but they still didn't understand. The disciples tried to change Jesus' mind about suffering and dying, but Jesus told them not to tempt him. It was God's Will that Jesus should come and die for our sins. Jesus came out of obedience to God. He came for the disciples and He came for us.

Palm Sunday

As the time drew near for Jesus to suffer for us, he traveled to Jerusalem. He told two of his disciples to go into a village and bring back a small donkey they would find there. Jesus said it would be a donkey that nobody had ever ridden. When his disciples found the donkey, they brought it to Jesus.

Jesus rode the little donkey into Jerusalem. The people of the city were very happy to see Jesus. They took off their cloaks and laid them across the road so the donkey could walk over them. They also cut branches from some palm trees, and waved the palms as Jesus rode past them. Everyone shouted, "Hosanna in the highest!"—which means "God, save us!" They said this because they thought Jesus had come to become their king.

The disciples told the people that Jesus was a prophet from Galilee. The high priests, who heard all of this, were angry and confused. They were also afraid. They knew that if all the people supported Jesus for their king instead of the Roman emperor, the Romans would be very angry. The priests were afraid the Romans would then come and punish the people and the priests.

The Last Supper

On Thursday, before the Passover feast, Jesus sent his apostles to prepare the Passover meal in the upstairs room of a house. When they were all gathered together, Jesus took a towel and washed the feet of each of his apostles. Peter did not want Jesus to wash his feet. He thought only servants should wash people's feet. But Jesus said that Peter must have his feet washed if he wanted to belong to God.

When Jesus finished washing the apostles' feet, he told them, "Do you understand what I just did for you? You call me 'Teacher' and 'Lord,' and that is what I am. But if I washed your feet, then you must wash each other's feet."

Jesus showed his followers that he had come not to be served, but to serve. Jesus was showing his apostles his love, so that they would pass his love on to others.

Then, during the meal, Jesus took the bread, blessed it, broke it, and gave it to his disciples saying, "Take and eat; this is My Body." Then he took a chalice of wine, gave thanks, and passed it around, saying, "Drink this, all of you, for this is My Blood, to be poured out for the forgiveness of sins. Do this in memory of me." This was the very first time that the apostles received Holy Communion, the Body and Blood of Jesus.

The Garden

After supper, Jesus went with his apostles to a garden that had many olive trees. Jesus told them to stay at the entrance to the garden, but he took Peter, James, and John into the garden with Him.

In the garden, Jesus prayed, asking God his Father to save him from what he knew was coming next. But he also said that he would do whatever God wanted. "Not my will," Jesus prayed, "but Yours, be done."

When he had finished praying, Jesus went to see his disciples, who were sleeping. He woke them and told them to watch and pray with him. Then Jesus returned where he had been before and continued to pray. He again visited his apostles, and found them still sleeping. Jesus felt very sad, because he had asked his apostles to pray with him three times, and three times he found them asleep.

Then Judas, one of the apostles, came into the Garden with the Jewish high priests and soldiers. Judas walked over to Jesus and kissed him. He betrayed Jesus. Then the soldiers knew that Jesus was the one they were going to arrest. They tied him up with ropes, and led him away. The apostles ran away in fear. They left Jesus all alone.

The Trial

The soldiers brought Jesus before the city leaders, who knew that Jesus was innocent. However, the high priests had hired men to lie about Jesus to the people.

The rulers asked Jesus if he was the Messiah and Jesus said yes. They were so angry with his answer that they demanded Jesus be killed. They dragged him before Pilate, the Roman governor.

Meanwhile, Peter was outside talking with some people who accused him of being a disciple of Jesus. They asked him three times and every time Peter denied knowing Jesus. The last time he denied it, a rooster crowed. When he heard it, Peter cried. Jesus had told him it would be so.

The soldiers brought Jesus to Pontius Pilate, the Roman governor. After questioning Jesus, Pilate decided that Jesus was innocent and that he should be set free. However, the crowd kept yelling, "Crucify Him!" Pilate had Jesus scourged and crowned with thorns. He did not want to kill Jesus.

The people demanded that Jesus be put to death. So Pilate washed his hands, as if to say, "I wash my hands of this. I am not responsible for what will happen next." He then gave the order for Jesus to be taken out and crucified.

Jesus Carries the Cross

The soldiers forced Jesus into the street. They laid a heavy wooden cross on his shoulders and made him carry it. On the way, Jesus met his Mother Mary. Mary felt very sad to see her beloved son suffer so much, yet she knew God had allowed this, in order for Jesus to save the whole world. She and Jesus looked at each other with great love and tears in their eyes. Then the guards pushed him on his way.

Because Jesus was so weak, he fell down. The soldiers made Simon, a man in the crowd, help carry Jesus' cross to Calvary, where Jesus would be killed. As they walked on together, they passed some women, who were crying for Jesus. Jesus told them, "Do not weep for me. Weep instead for yourselves and for your children. If these things happen to me, what will happen to you?"

When Jesus got to the small hill of Calvary, the soldiers nailed him to the cross between two thieves. One of the thieves made fun of Jesus. However, the other said they deserved what was happening to them, but Jesus had done nothing wrong. Then he said, "Jesus, remember me when you come into your kingdom." Jesus replied, "Surely I tell you, today you will be with me in Paradise."

Jesus Dies on the Cross

As Jesus hung on the cross, suspended only by two nails in his hands and two nails in his feet, some soldiers noticed he was thirsty. They offered him a sponge they had soaked in wine, but Jesus refused to drink.

Many people who saw Jesus hanging there called him names and made fun of him. The soldiers made a sign that they put above Jesus on the cross. It read, "Jesus of Nazareth, King of the Jews." They did not really believe in him. They were mocking him and making fun of him just like most of the other people.

Jesus prayed out loud to God, "Forgive them, Father, for they do not know what they are doing." Then he looked down on his Mother Mary and his beloved disciple John. Jesus said to Mary, "Woman, behold your son." He then said to John, "Son, behold your mother." From that day on, John took Mary into his home and cared for her.

Finally, after three hours of agony, Jesus said, "It is finished. Father, into Your hands I commit my spirit." He breathed one last time. Then, bowing his head, Jesus died.

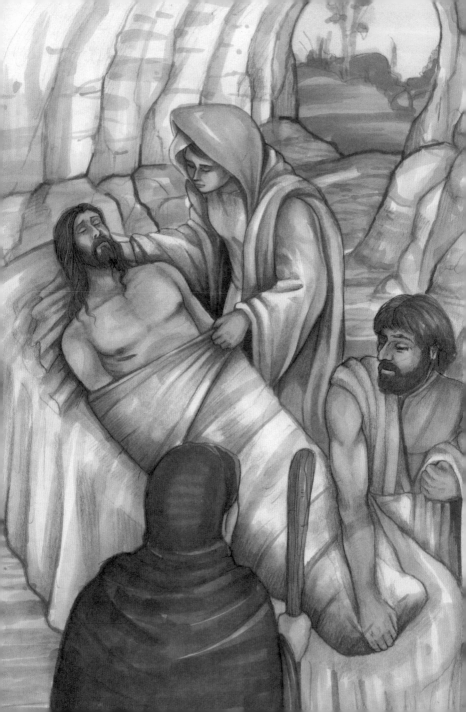

Jesus is Buried

A wealthy man named Joseph of Arimathea, a secret disciple of Jesus, asked Pilate for permission to remove the body of Jesus from the cross. Pilate gave him permission, so he and some of the disciples took Jesus' body down from the cross. Mother Mary felt great sorrow as she held Jesus in her arms one last time. Then Mary and some women and some other disciples, including a man named Nicodemus, prepared Jesus' body for burial. They cleaned it and wrapped it in clean linen and sweet spices. However, they did not have time to anoint his body with oil. They buried Jesus in the tomb of Joseph of Arimathea which had just been carved in a rock. Then Joseph rolled a huge stone across the entrance to the tomb and all the disciples departed. However, Mary Magdalene and another Mary remained there, facing the tomb.

The next day the chief priests went to Pilate, and asked for soldiers to guard the tomb, since Jesus had said he would rise on the third day. They were afraid Jesus' disciples might come and take his body and tell people that Jesus had risen from the dead. Pilate said, "The guard is yours. Go guard the tomb as best you can." The priests went and sealed the tomb. But as we shall see, God had other plans.

Jesus Rises from the Dead!

Very early in the morning on the first day of the week, the earth began to quake. An angel of the Lord came down from heaven and rolled away the stone from the tomb. Suddenly, in a burst of great light, Jesus arose from the dead! He shined brighter than the sun rising after a dark night. The soldiers cried out and ran away in fear.

Just after sunrise that morning, Mary Magdalene and some women went out to the place where they buried Jesus, so they could finish anointing Jesus' body with oil.

To their great surprise, they saw that the tomb entrance was open. "The stone is rolled away!" they cried. They ran down to the tomb, but did not find the body of Jesus. Then an angel appeared, and told them, "Do not be afraid! I know you are seeking Jesus the crucified. He is not here, for He is risen, just as He said. Come and see the place where He lay. Then go tell His disciples that He has been raised from the dead."

The women left the tomb quickly, afraid yet overjoyed. They ran to tell the good news to Peter and the other disciples.

Jesus Meets Mary Magdalene

The women were excited and ran to tell the disciples the news, but Mary Magdalene was still very sad, and she stayed outside the tomb weeping and mourning for her Lord. She loved Jesus very much and had suffered greatly when she saw Him die on the cross. She turned around and saw a man standing near her. "Woman," He said, "why are you weeping? Who are you looking for?" Thinking He was the gardener, Mary replied, "Sir, if you carried my Lord away, tell me where you laid him, and I will take him." The man was Jesus.

"Mary!" he said. Mary turned to Jesus and exclaimed, "Rabbi!" Then she went to embrace Him. Jesus said to her, "Stop holding on to Me, for I have not yet ascended to the Father. But go to My brothers and tell them, 'I am going to My Father and to your Father, to My God and to your God!'"

Mary left, overjoyed, and ran to the disciples. "I have seen the Lord!" she proclaimed. Then she told Peter and all the apostles and disciples the amazing news that Jesus had risen from the dead!

Jesus Appears to His Disciples

On the evening of the Resurrection, the apostles were gathered in the upper room. The doors were locked for fear of the Jews, when suddenly, Jesus came and stood among them. "Peace be with you!" He said. He showed them His hands and His side. Then He said, "As the Father has sent Me, so I now send you."

Jesus breathed on them and said, "Receive the Holy Spirit. Whose sins you shall forgive are forgiven them, and whose sins you shall hold back, they are held back."

Thomas was not with the other apostles that night. When the apostles told him they had seen Jesus, he said, "Unless I put my finger into the nail marks in His hands and put my hand into His side, I will not believe."

A week later, Thomas was with the disciples inside the locked room. Suddenly, Jesus came and stood among them, and said, "Peace be with you!" Then He said to Thomas, "Place your finger into My hands and put your hand into My side, and do not be unbelieving, but believe." Thomas gasped in amazement. He knelt down and cried, "My Lord and my God!"

The Road to Emmaus

On the Sunday of the Resurrection, two disciples were walking from Jerusalem to a village named Emmaus. These men had not seen the risen Jesus, and as far as they knew, Jesus was dead. They were very sad and could not understand why Jesus had to die.

Jesus walked up to them and started talking with them, but they did not recognize Him. They told Him that they had heard that Jesus had risen from the dead, but that none of it made any sense to them. Jesus said, "How foolish you are! How slow of heart to believe!" He explained that the Scriptures had foretold that the Messiah, or Christ, had to suffer these things and enter into His glory. Then, beginning with Moses and the other prophets, Jesus told the two men about all the prophecies that spoke of Him.

When they reached the village, the disciples asked the stranger to stay with them. While they were eating, Jesus broke the bread, blessed it, and gave it to them. Suddenly they understood that the stranger was Jesus! Then Jesus disappeared. He vanished from their sight, but their hearts were burning with love because He had spoken with them. They were joyful because Jesus had risen from the dead!

The Ascension of the Lord

For 40 days after His Resurrection, Jesus appeared to His disciples. Then He asked His apostles to follow him to a hillside outside Jerusalem. When they arrived there, Jesus told them, "All power in heaven and on earth has been given to Me. Go therefore, and make disciples of all the nations, of all people who speak in every language, all over the world. Tell them that I died for them and arose from the dead to save them from their sins, so they can live forever in heaven with Me.

"Tell all the people to believe that I am God's only Son, the one whom God sent into the world. When you make disciples, baptize them in the name of the Father, and of the Son and of the Holy Spirit."

Jesus then raised His hands and blessed His disciples. As He blessed them, He parted from them and was taken up into the clouds! He went up into heaven where He sits now at the right hand of God the Father.

After Jesus had gone into heaven, two angels appeared beside the apostles. They told them that Jesus would return in the same way as they saw Him go into heaven. Then the apostles returned to Jerusalem, to pray for the coming of the Holy Spirit.

Pentecost

Ten days later, Mother Mary, the apostles, and the other disciples were gathered together in one room. Suddenly, they heard the sound of a mighty wind that shook the room. Flames that looked like tongues of fire appeared over their heads. This was the Holy Spirit, the Comforter that Jesus had told them about!

In a very special way, the Holy Spirit, who is the Fire of God and the Third Person of the Blessed Trinity, had come to live in the hearts of His people. Those who believed that Jesus was the Son of God received this gift of the Holy Spirit on the feast of Pentecost.

All the disciples were filled with such courage and enthusiasm that they began preaching about Jesus' death and resurrection. A huge crowd of people from many different lands had gathered to see what caused the noise. They were astonished to realize that no matter where they came from or what language they spoke, they understood what the apostles were saying!

The Holy Spirit made this miracle happen. Saint Peter preached about Jesus, and over 3,000 people believed in Jesus' name and were baptized that very day. The Church was born!

The Return of Jesus

The Bible tells us that Jesus will return to us again some day, in the same way as He left us, in a cloud of glory. He will come as a Savior to raise the dead to life, and to gather up all of God's children to be with Him in heaven forever.

Jesus will return as a great King and Warrior, in glory and splendor. He will defeat the devil forever, and He will judge all people. We do not know when this will happen, but it is important that we prepare for His coming and honor Him by obeying Him and our parents, by praying to God and by loving other people.

Jesus wants us to share in His love now by receiving the Sacraments, especially by going to Mass and receiving the Eucharist, which we call Holy Communion. During the Mass, when the priest says the words of Jesus at the Last Supper, a miracle takes place and the bread becomes the actual Body of Jesus and the wine becomes His Blood. In Holy Communion, we meet Jesus and take Him into our hearts. Until the day that Jesus returns in all His glory and majesty, the Church will celebrate this wonderful Day of Mystery. Go, tell others that Jesus is coming again! Celebrate and be happy for all the wonderful things our God and Savior has done for us. Jesus is Lord!

The Day of the Lord

Sunday is the most special day of our week, because God commands us to keep it as a holy day. We come together on Sunday to be with others who believe in Jesus and to remember and reflect on all the things God has done for us. We worship God the Father, the Son, and the Holy Spirit at Holy Mass. Every Sunday is like a little Easter, for on this day we gather to celebrate the Resurrection of Jesus from the dead. We remember how He loved us, and died for our sins, so that we could become the children of God and enter the Kingdom of Heaven. Praise God!